DINOSAUR DISCOVERIES

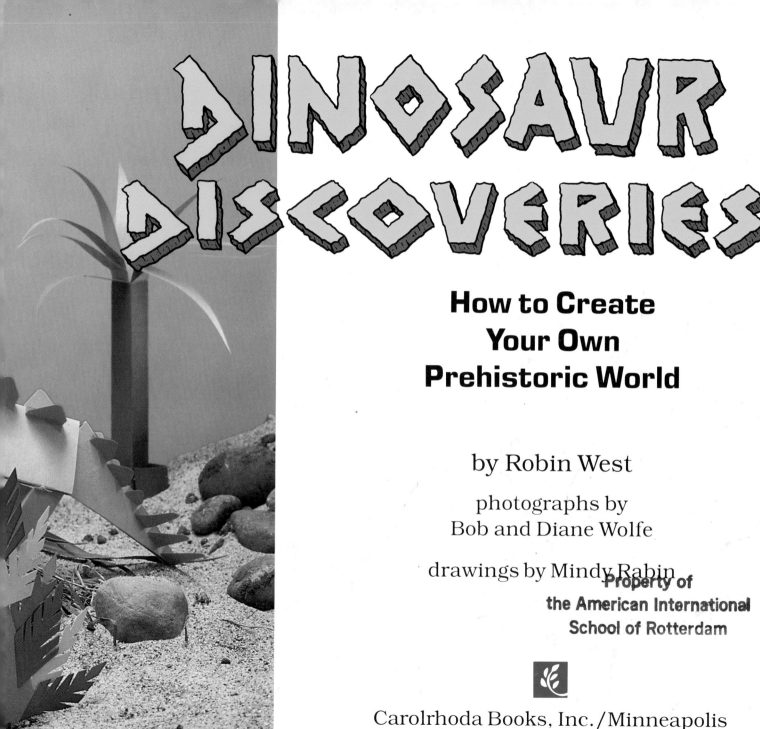

DINOSAUR DISCOVERIES

How to Create Your Own Prehistoric World

by Robin West

photographs by
Bob and Diane Wolfe

drawings by Mindy Rabin

Carolrhoda Books, Inc./Minneapolis

To Porky and Marbs

Library of Congress Cataloging-in-Publication Data

West, Robin.
        Dinosaur discoveries : how to create your own prehistoric world/
by Robin West : photographs by Bob and Diane Wolfe : drawings by
Mindy Rabin.
        p.   cm.
        Summary: Instructions for drawing, cutting and gluing paper
shapes together to form three-dimensional dinosaurs.
        ISBN 0-87614-351-6
        1. Paper work—Juvenile literature. 2. Dinosaurs—Juvenile
literature.   [1. Paper work. 2. Handicraft. 3. Dinosaurs.]
I. Wolfe, Robert L., ill. II. Wolfe, Diane, ill. III. Rabin,
Mindy, ill. IV. Title.
TT870.W45 1989
745.54—dc19   88-32513
                                                                      CIP
                                                                       AC

3   4   5   6   7   8   9   10   98   97   96   95   94   93   92   91   90

Contents

Dear Reader,

Come along with Molly, Kirby, and Marbles as they explore a land where dinosaurs roam free. Then, using materials you can find around the house, make your own prehistoric world by drawing, cutting, and gluing shapes together to form three-dimensional creatures. My ideas and suggestions may spark your imagination and encourage you to design your very own dinosaur characters. You'll be amazed at how circles, triangles, squares, and rectangles can come together to create these incredible beasts!

The directions are easy to follow. Each project is divided into simple steps. For example, if you are making Stanley Stegosaurus, you will find sections of directions for his body, legs, head, and tail, as well as some decorating tips to make Stanley more lifelike. As you work your way through the book, you'll gain the skills you'll need for the more challenging projects at the back of the book.

The projects in this book take you to another time and place, so don't be afraid to use your imagination. Much is known about the prehistoric world of dinosaurs, but there is still plenty left for you to discover.

When you have decided what you want to make, read all the instructions carefully before you begin. Then gather all the materials you will need. You will probably want to work on old newspapers so that glue or paint spills won't matter. Be sure to ask for help if you need it. Above all, have fun making and playing with your prehistoric world!

Your Basic Equipment:

colored construction paper
pencil
ruler
scissors
white liquid glue
Elmer's glue is fine.
clear-drying glue
This can be found in a fabric or hobby store. Super Tacky glue works well.
masking tape
colored felt-tip markers
paper punch
This is not necessary but is nice to have to make perfect circles for the dinosaurs' eyes.

Things To Save:

cans
Save sizes 10 ounce, 15 ounce, and 32 ounce. Make sure one lid is removed and each can is clean.
string
yarn
pipe cleaners
toilet paper tubes
large and small thread spools

Equipment You Will Need for Only a Few Projects:

paper fasteners
a few small- and medium-sized nails
wooden non-clip clothespin
spray paint
wire clothes hanger
hammer
wire clipper
fishing line or transparent thread
tracing paper

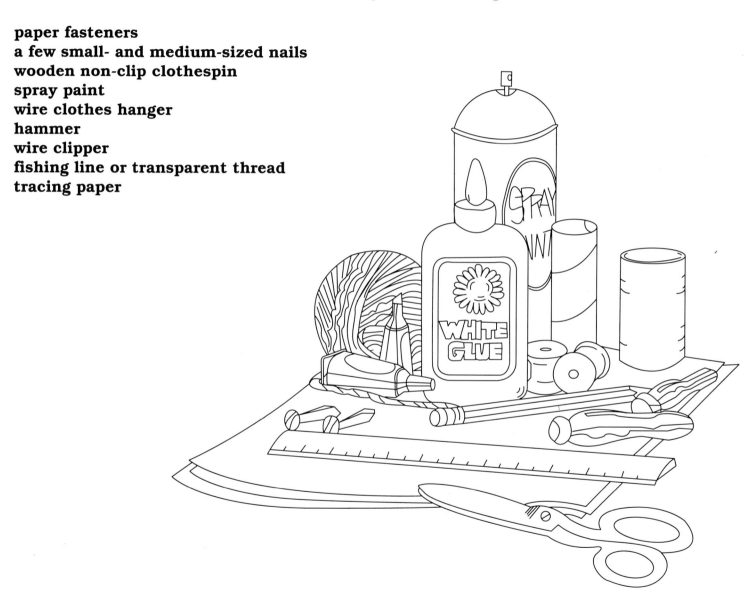

colored construction paper
pencil
scissors
white liquid glue
clear-drying glue
colored felt-tip markers
yarn
2 small thread spools
tracing paper

Molly, Kirby, and Marbles

Hi! I'm Molly. This is my cousin Kirby. The big beast standing beside us is Marbles, the wonder dog. We have an incredible story to share with you.

It all started one morning as Kirby and I took Marbles for a walk in the park. It *seemed* like an ordinary day. The birds were singing, the sky was blue, and we were all in fine spirits as we strolled along. Suddenly, out of a thicket came a big brown squirrel. Without a moment's hesitation, Marbles chased after the furry creature. Kirby and I took off in hot pursuit. We didn't think twice about following him through a hole in the fence — until we got to the other side.

Before you join us in our adventure, take a minute to put us together. We promise you will have the time of your life discovering dinosaurs!

8

Let's Begin:

Molly and Kirby

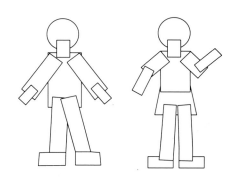

1. On this page are life-sized patterns of the shapes used to make Molly and Kirby. To make your own patterns, trace over the figures on this page onto tracing paper. Then cut out what you have traced. Lay these tracing-paper patterns on a piece of construction paper and draw around them. Cut out your final pieces from the construction paper.
2. Glue the pieces together with white liquid glue as pictured above.

For Molly & Kirby

hand (cut 4)   head (cut 2)   neck (cut 2)

How I Decorated:

You can draw Molly and Kirby's faces with a felt-tip marker. Glue pieces of yarn to their heads for hair. Use your imagination to decorate their clothes. When you have completed Molly and Kirby, glue their backs to the top rim of the thread spools with clear-drying glue.

For Molly

shirt   skirt   shoe (cut 2)   belt   leg (cut 2)

For Kirby

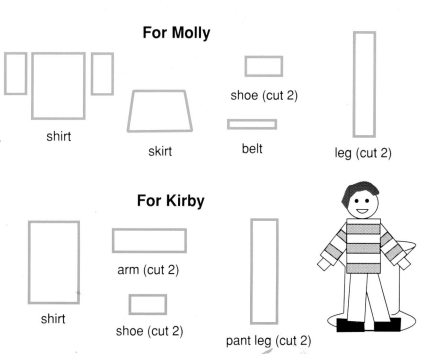

shirt   arm (cut 2)   shoe (cut 2)   pant leg (cut 2)

Marbles

1. Trace the patterns for Marbles's head and body onto tracing paper. Cut out what you have traced. Lay your tracing-paper patterns on a folded piece of construction paper so the side with the dotted line is on the fold, and draw around them. Cut out your final pieces from the construction paper, being careful not to cut on the folded side.
2. Glue the head to the body as pictured.

How I Decorated:

I cut out spots, ears, eyes, and a tail from construction paper and glued them to Marbles's body. Because Marbles's body was cut on the fold, he can stand all on his own.

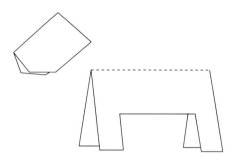

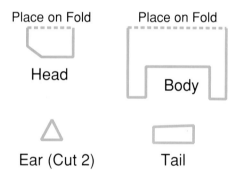

Place on Fold   Place on Fold

Head   Body

Ear (Cut 2)   Tail

You Will Need:

colored construction paper
pencil
scissors
white liquid glue
clear-drying glue
colored felt-tip markers
1 wooden non-clip clothespin
tracing paper

Milly Meganeura

We heard Milly Meganeura coming before we saw her. The immense colorful wings of this dragonfly-like insect created quite a hum as she flew by us!

Let's Begin:

1. Milly is made by attaching a double set of wings to a clothespin. To make the wings, trace Figure A on this page onto tracing paper, and cut it out to make the pattern. Lay your tracing-paper pattern on a folded piece of construction paper so the side with the dotted line is on the fold, and draw around it. Cut out your final piece, being careful not to cut on the folded side. Make a second set of wings in the same way.

Figure A

Place on fold

2. Glue both wings to the underside of the clothespin with clear-drying glue.

How I Decorated:

I glued many different shapes and colors of construction paper to Milly's wings. Felt-tip markers work well for decorating the body. Use your imagination and create a beautiful meganeura, unlike all others!

colored construction paper
pencil
ruler
scissors
white liquid glue
clear-drying glue
1 pipe cleaner
1 toilet paper tube
1 thread spool
1 small nail
fishing line or transparent thread
tracing paper

Roberta Rhamphorhynchus

With her reptilian teeth and powerful wings, Roberta Rhamphorhynchus is an impressive creature of the skies. We watched as she soared higher and higher.

Let's Begin:

The Body

1. The body is made by cutting a toilet paper tube into a $2^1/_2$-inch length. Discard the shorter end.
2. Draw and cut out from construction paper a rectangle $2^1/_2$ inches high by 6 inches wide.

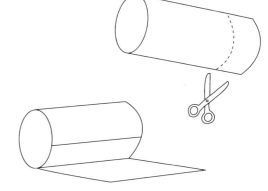

3. Glue the short end of the rectangle to the side of the tube and wrap it around the tube. Fasten the end with glue.

The Wings

1. Make a pattern for the wings by drawing and cutting out a rectangle 3 inches high by 8 inches wide.
2. From corners C and D, measure up 1 inch and mark each point with a dot.

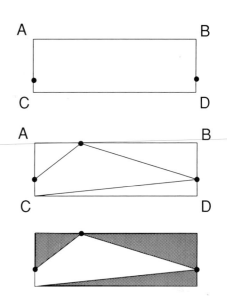

3. From corner A, measure $2^1/_2$ inches over on the upper edge and mark this point with a dot. Connect the dots and corner as shown.
4. Cut off the areas shaded in the diagram and discard them. You now have your wing pattern.

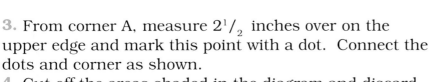

5. For the actual wings, you will need two pieces of paper at least 3 inches high by 16 inches wide. Fold each piece of paper in half.

6. Place the pattern on the fold as shown. Trace around the pattern. Do this on each piece of paper.

7. Cut out the shapes you traced. Be careful not to cut on the folded edges.

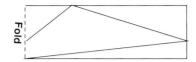

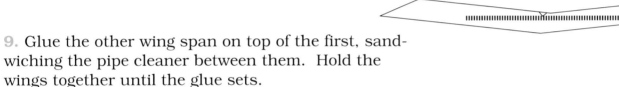

8. Glue a pipe cleaner to the back of one of the wing spans, using clear-drying glue for the best results.

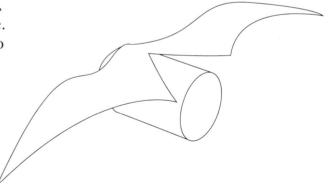

9. Glue the other wing span on top of the first, sandwiching the pipe cleaner between them. Hold the wings together until the glue sets.

10. Glue the wing span to the back edge of the body, carefully molding the center wing section to the tube. Gently bend the wings up and down on either side to give them the appearance of flight.

The Head

1. To make the head, trace Figure B on tracing paper, and cut it out to make a pattern. Then draw a line around the pattern on construction paper and cut it out.

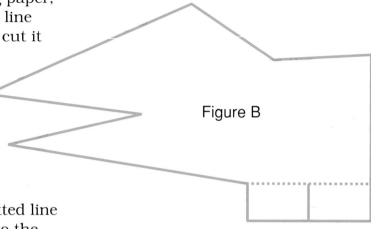

Figure B

2. Using the pattern as a guide, fold on the dotted line to form a tab. Snip on the short solid line up to the dotted line. Fold tabs in opposite directions.

3. Apply glue to the outside edges of the tabs you just made and slide the head into the body tube. Press the tabs down into the bottom of the body tube.

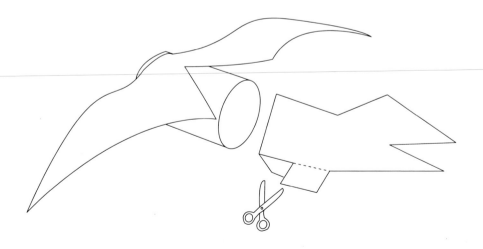

The Tail

1. To make the tail, trace all solid and dotted lines of Figure C on tracing paper, and cut it out to make a pattern. Then trace around the pattern onto construction paper and cut it out.

2. Lay your tracing-paper pattern on top of the construction paper piece. Using the pattern as a guide, fold on the dotted lines to make tabs for the tail. Fold one tab up and the other tab down.

3. Apply glue to the outside edges of the tabs, and slide them into the back end of the body. Attach one tab to the top of the tube and the other to the bottom. Hold the tabs in place until the glue sets.

The Legs

1. Figure D on this page is the leg pattern. Trace, draw, and cut out the legs in the same way you did the head and tail.

2. Apply glue to the back side of each leg and attach to the lower half of the tube on each side — toward the back under the wings.

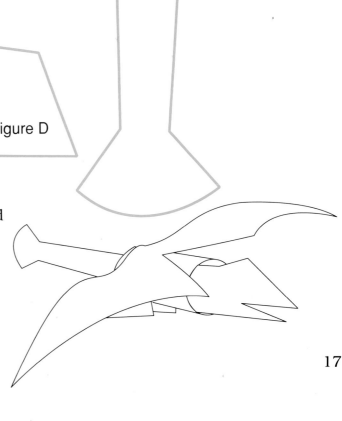

Figure C

Figure D

17

How I Decorated:

I made claw feet and hands for Roberta. Glue hand claws to the front center tips of the wings and foot claws to the back tips of the legs. You can use my patterns or make your own. Don't forget to make her eyes and sharp teeth.

Flying

1. Roberta will fly if you follow a few simple directions. Use a nail to punch two small holes in the top front of the body, one on either side of the center line made by the head. Punch a third hole in the center of the top at the back end. This hole will go through the wings. Be careful, because a nail can be very sharp.
2. Cut two pieces of fishing line, each 24 inches long.

3. Thread each piece of fishing line down through one of the front holes. Then thread both pieces of fishing line up through the back hole.
4. Slide both pieces of fishing line through the large thread spool. Tie the ends of the fishing line together and knot securely.

5. To make Roberta fly, slide a long piece of string through the thread spool. Attach one end of the string to a chair and the other end to a lower point across the room. Stand back and watch her zoom!

Foot claw

Hand claw

You Will Need:

colored construction paper
pencil
ruler
scissors
white liquid glue

Stanley Stegosaurus

When we met Stanley he was munching on some
shrubbery, which was natural for a plant-eater like
the stegosaurus. Notice his protective armor
plates. He doesn't need to worry about hostile
advances from us!

Let's Begin:

The Body

1. Draw and cut out a rectangle 5 inches high by 8 inches wide. Fold the paper in half and crease. Fold the paper in half again and make another crease.
2. Open up the paper and form it into a triangle by overlapping the two end segments.
3. Glue the overlapped ends together. The glued side will be the underside of the triangle-shaped body.

The Legs

1. Let's make the back legs first. Draw and cut out two rectangles $2^1/_2$ inches high by 4 inches wide. Fold each paper in half. Then fold each paper in half again. Form a triangle from each piece by overlapping the end segments and gluing them together.
2. At one end of each leg, make a $1/_4$-inch cut along two of the creases. Fold out the cut portions to form tabs.
3. Fold out the two remaining sides of each triangle to form two more tabs. Set these legs aside for now.
4. To make the shorter front legs, draw and cut out two rectangles 2 inches high by 4 inches wide. Make a triangle from each piece the same way you made the back legs.
5. Follow steps 2 and 3 in forming the tabs for the front legs.

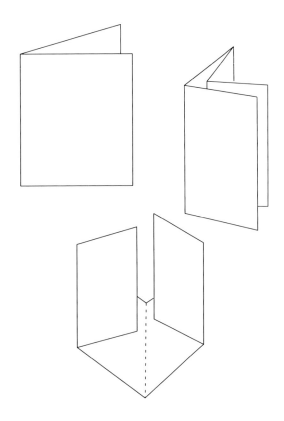

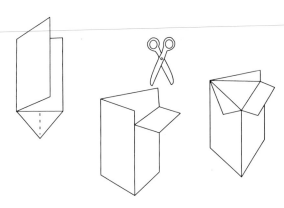

6. Apply glue to all tabs on the front and back legs. Glue these tabs to the bottom of the body. Make sure you glue the longer legs to the back end and the shorter legs to the front end. Stanley should now be leaning forward.

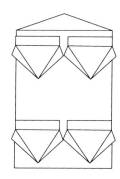

The Head

1. Draw and cut out a rectangle 4 inches high by 8 inches wide. Fold the paper in half and crease.
2. Unfold the paper. Along the bottom edge, measure out 2 inches from the folded center line on both sides and mark each point with a dot.

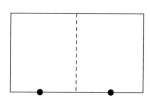

3. Draw a diagonal line from each dot to the top of the folded center line to form a triangle.
4. From each bottom corner, draw a diagonal line up to the top of the folded center line to form an even larger triangle.
5. Measure $1/2$ inch down from the top edge of the paper on both sides and mark each point with a dot.

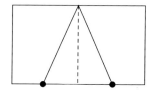

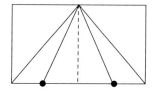  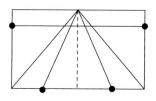

6. Connect these last two dots to make a horizontal line.
7. Cut off the areas shaded in the diagram and discard these pieces.

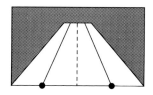

8. Fold on each of the diagonal lines. Form the shape into a triangle by overlapping the end segments. Glue the overlapped ends together. This is Stanley's head and long snout.

9. To attach the head to the body, apply glue to the overlapped side of the head and slide it about an inch into the front end of the body. Hold this in place until the glue sets.

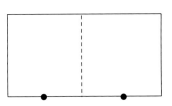

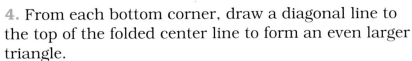

The Tail

1. Draw and cut out a rectangle 5 inches high by 8 inches wide. Fold the paper in half and crease.

2. Unfold the paper. Along the bottom edge, measure 2 inches from the folded center line on both sides and mark each point with a dot.

3. Draw a diagonal line from each dot to the top of the folded center line to form a triangle.

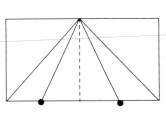

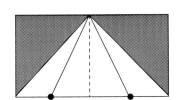

4. From each bottom corner, draw a diagonal line to the top of the folded center line to form an even larger triangle.

5. Cut off the areas shaded in the diagram and discard these pieces.

6. Make a crease on each of the diagonal lines. Form the shape into a triangle by overlapping the two end segments. Glue the overlapped ends together. This will be the underside of the tail.

7. To attach the tail to the body, apply glue to the underside of the tail and slide it about an inch into the back end of the body. Hold the tail in place until the glue sets.

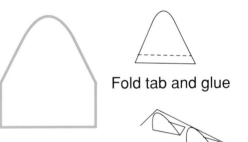

How I Decorated:

An important feature of Stanley's body, head, and tail is the protective plates. I cut small, medium, and large triangles out of different-colored construction paper. I formed tabs by folding the bottom edges of the triangles. I glued the tabs close to the "spine," or top edge of the body, and folded them upwards so the plates covered the tabs. You may notice my triangles don't look pointy. I rounded the edges to give the plates a more realistic look. I finished Stanley by gluing circles of construction paper together for his eyes.

Fold tab and glue

Claws

You Will Need:

colored construction paper
pencil
ruler
scissors
white liquid glue
masking tape
1 toilet paper tube
tracing paper

Dimitri Dimetrodon

Dimitri is a most unusual and beautiful creature. He has a fantastic sailback fin for cooling his body during long, hot days. We were delighted by his vivid purple color and friendly smile.

24

Let's Begin:

The Body

1. Draw and cut out a rectangle 4 $\frac{1}{2}$ inches high by 6 inches wide. Glue the short end of the rectangle to the side of the toilet paper tube, and wrap it around the tube. Fasten the end with glue.

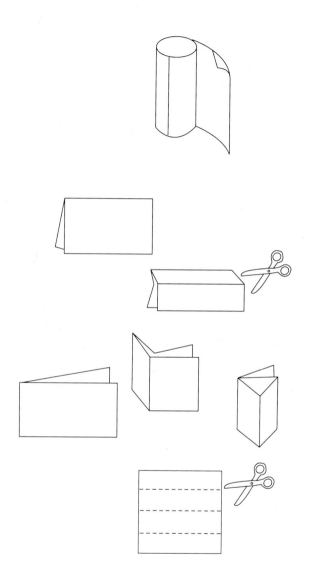

The Legs

1. Each leg has an upper and lower section. To make the lower leg sections, draw and cut out a rectangle 6 inches high by 4 inches wide. Fold the paper in half. Fold the paper in half again. Open the paper, and cut on the three fold lines to make four strips 1 $\frac{1}{2}$ inches high by 4 inches wide.

2. Fold each strip in half. Fold each one in half again.
3. Open each strip and form it into a triangle by overlapping the end segments and gluing them together.
4. To make the upper leg sections, draw and cut out a square 4 inches high by 4 inches wide. Fold and cut the square into four strips the same way you did in step one. You will end up with four small rectangles 1 inch high by 4 inches wide.

5. Fold and glue these strips into triangles the same way you made the lower legs.

6. At this point, let's attach the legs to the body. Draw and cut out two rectangles 1 inch high by 4 inches wide.

7. Apply glue to each end of the strips of paper. Slide a leg section onto each end of the strips of paper, and hold until set. Allow 2 inches in between the sections.

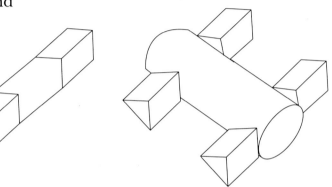

8. Apply glue to the space between the sections on each strip. Glue one strip to each end of the body.

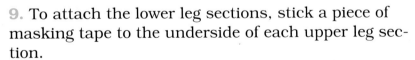

9. To attach the lower leg sections, stick a piece of masking tape to the underside of each upper leg section.

10. Fold the pieces of tape down to form tabs, and stick them to the insides of the lower leg sections. The tape makes a hinge so the lower section sits under the upper section.

The Head

1. Trace Figure E on tracing paper and cut it out to make a pattern. Then trace around the pattern on construction paper and cut it out.
2. To attach the head to the body, make a $^1/_2$-inch slit in the top of the body tube. Slide the head into the slit.

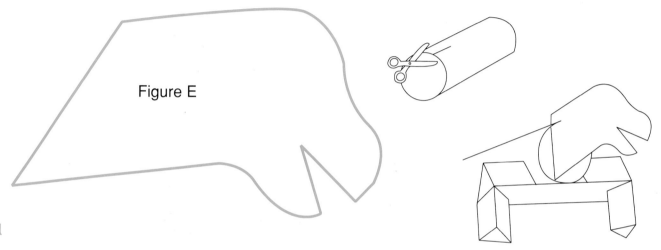

Figure E

The Tail

1. Dimitri needs a tail, so don't forget to make him one. Draw and cut out a rectangle 5 inches high by 6 inches wide. Fold the rectangle in half.
2. Open the rectangle. Along the bottom edge, measure out $1^1/_2$ inches from the folded center line on both sides and mark these points with dots.

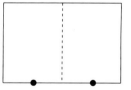

3. Draw two diagonal lines from these dots up to the top of the folded center line to form a triangle.

4. From each bottom corner, draw a diagonal line up to the top of the folded center line to form a larger triangle. Cut off the areas shaded in the diagram, and discard these pieces.

5. Fold the sides of the triangle in on the diagonal lines you drew. Form the shape into a triangle by overlapping the end segments and gluing them together.

6. Slide the tail up into the body slightly, and attach the tail to the inside of the body with masking tape.

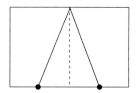

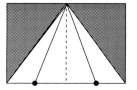

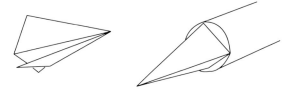

The Fin

1. The finishing feature of the dimetrodon is its fin. Place a circular object about 5 inches in diameter (a full roll of masking tape will work) on a piece of paper. Draw a line around the outside of the object.

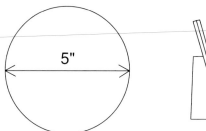

5"

2. Cut out the circle and fold it in half.

3. Fold it in half again. (The point where the two fold lines meet is the center point.) Mark the center point with a dot.

4. Draw a line $\frac{1}{2}$ inch below a fold line.

5. From the end points of the line you just drew, draw two diagonal lines up to the center point.

6. Cut off the area shaded in the diagram and discard it.

7. To create the fan effect, start at one side and fold the paper back and forth on top of itself all the way around the half circle.

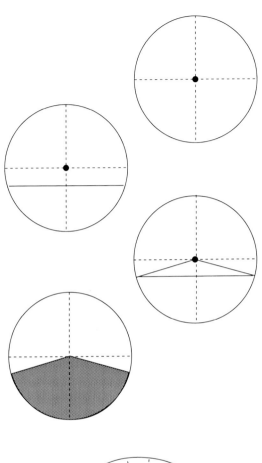

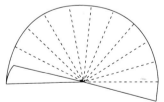

8. To attach the fin to the body, apply glue to the last folded section on each side of the fin. Press these sections to the top of the body, one on either side of the center, and hold them until the glue sets.

9. Glue the fin to Dimitri's head to secure his head to his body.

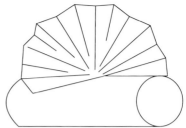

How I Decorated:

Dimitri has small triangular toes and teeth. I used circles and small triangles to make his eyes. Can you come up with something different and interesting?

Toes   Teeth

You Will Need:

colored construction paper
pencil
ruler
scissors
white liquid glue
masking tape

Lydia Leidyosuchus

Lydia has quite a last name! Can you pronounce it? Let's just call this crocodilian creature by her first name. Although she sports a rather large set of teeth, she was relaxed and contented as she sunned herself near the marsh.

31

Let's Begin:

The Body

1. Draw and cut out a rectangle 5 inches high by 6 inches wide. Measure $1^1/_2$ inches in from the sides on the upper and lower edges. Mark these points with dots.
2. Draw lines connecting these dots as shown.
3. Fold on the lines you just made to make the flaps that form the bottom of Lydia's body.
4. Form this shape into a three-dimensional half circle, overlapping the end segments and gluing them together.

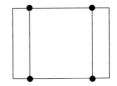

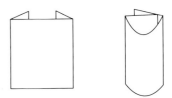

The Legs

1. For Lydia's legs, draw and cut out a rectangle 4 inches high by 8 inches wide. Fold this paper in half. Fold it in half again. Fold it in half one more time. Open the paper and cut on the seven fold lines. You should have eight pieces 4 inches high by 1 inch wide.

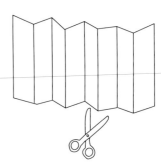

2. Fold each of these strips in half. Fold the strips in half again.

3. Open each strip and form it into a triangle by overlapping the end segments and gluing them together.

4. At this point, let's attach the legs to the body. First, draw and cut out two rectangles 1 inch high by $3\,^1/_2$ inches wide.

5. Apply glue to each end of the strips of paper. Slide a leg section onto each end of the strips of paper and hold until set. Make sure the legs are at least $1\,^1/_2$ inches apart on the strips.

6. Apply glue to the middle of the strips, and set the flat side of the body between the legs so one leg strip is at the front and one is at the back of the body.

7. To attach the lower leg portions, stick a piece of masking tape underneath each upper leg triangle.

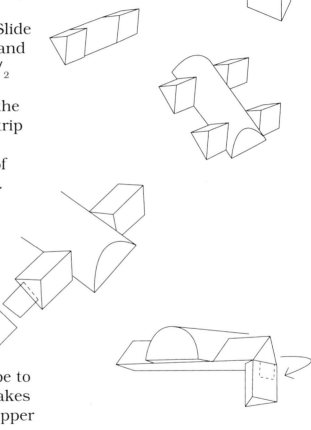

8. Fold the tape down to form tabs. Stick the tape to the insides of the lower leg triangles. The tape makes a hinge so that the lower triangle sits under the upper triangle.

The Head

1. Draw and cut out a rectangle 3 inches high by 6 inches wide. Find the center of this rectangle by measuring 3 inches from one side on the top and bottom edges. Mark these points with dots.

2. Along the top edge of the rectangle, measure 1 inch from either side of the center dot and mark each point with a dot.

3. Measure 2 inches out from either side of the center dot and mark these points with dots.

4. Along the bottom of the rectangle, measure $1^1/_2$ inches from either side of the center dot and mark each point with a dot.

5. Connect dots as shown: the bottom corners to upper-outside dots, lower-inside dots to upper-inside dots.

6. Cut off the areas that are shaded in the diagram and discard these pieces.

7. Fold the paper on lines A and B. Shape the paper into a tapered, three-dimensional half circle by over-lapping the end segments and gluing them together.

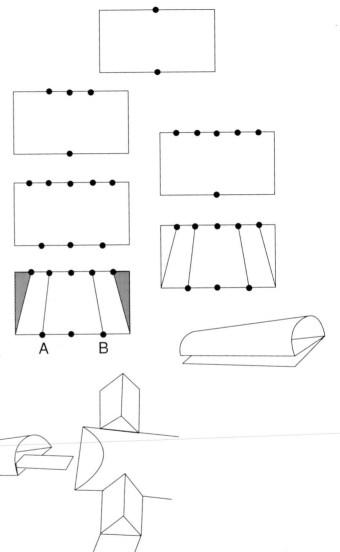

8. Sliding the head into the body slightly, attach the head to the body using masking tape.

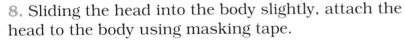

The Tail

1. Lydia's tail is made in much the same way as her head. Draw and cut out a square 6 inches high by 6 inches wide. Find the center of the square by measuring in 3 inches from the side on the top and bottom edges. Mark each point with a dot.

2. Along the top edge of the square, measure $1/2$ inch from either side of the center dot and mark each point with a dot.

3. Measure another $1/2$ inch out from the two dots you just made and mark each of these points with a dot.

4. Along the bottom edge of the square, measure out $1^1/_2$ inches on either side of the center dot and mark each point with a dot.

5. Connect the dots as shown: bottom corners to upper-outside dots, lower-inside dots to upper-inside dots.

6. Cut off the areas shaded in the diagram and discard these pieces.

7. Fold the paper on lines A and B. Shape the paper into a three-dimensional half circle by overlapping the end segments and gluing them together. Attach the tail by placing one end of a piece of masking tape inside the body's back bottom edge and the other end inside the front bottom edge of the tail. The tape will act as a hinge.

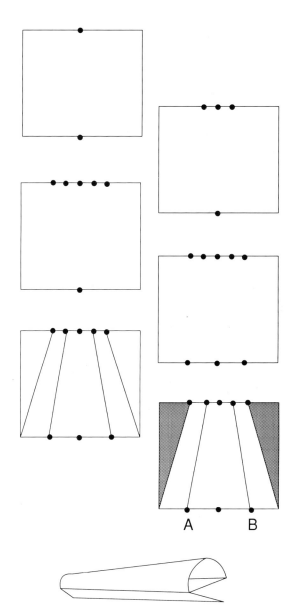

A   B

How I Decorated:

I gave Lydia sharp teeth and claws by cutting out
small pointy triangles and gluing them to the outside
of Lydia's head and feet. I also added lips and made
interesting eyes by cutting three sizes of circles and
gluing one on top of the other. Add some other clever
details of your own.

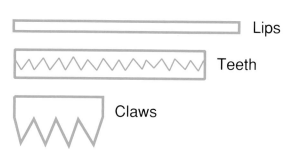

Lips

Teeth

Claws

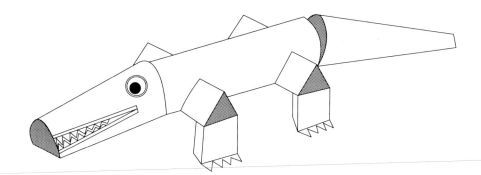

colored construction paper
pencil
ruler
scissors
white liquid glue
1 32-ounce clean can with
   1 lid removed

Trudy Triceratops

The horns projecting from Trudy's head make her a
wild-looking beast. But looks can be deceiving.
She was quite friendly as we passed by her.

Let's Begin:

The Body

1. Draw and cut out a rectangle $4^3/_4$ inches high by 14 inches wide.
2. Glue the short end of the rectangle to the side of the can and wrap it around the can. Fasten the end with glue.
3. Place the end of the can on a piece of paper and draw a line around the outside of the can. Cut out this circle.
4. Glue the circle to the can's lid.

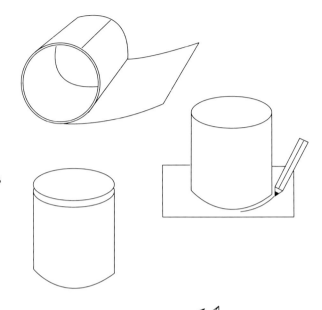

The Legs

1. Draw and cut out a piece of paper 6 inches high by 12 inches wide. Fold the paper in half and crease. Fold it in half again and crease. Fold it in half one more time and crease. Unfold the paper and cut on the folds. You now have eight 6- by $1^1/_2$- inch rectangles.
2. Glue the ends of each rectangle together to form eight tubes $1^1/_2$ inches tall.

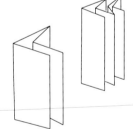

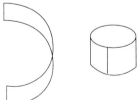

3. Using masking tape, attach four of the tubes to the bottom side of the body. Fasten one end of masking tape to the inside of the tube and the other end to the bottom of the can. These are the upper leg sections.

4. The four remaining tubes are the lower leg sections. Attach them to the upper leg sections using one piece of masking tape like a hinge connecting only the inner sides. The upper leg sections should sit on top of the lower leg sections at an angle so Trudy can stand flat on the ground.

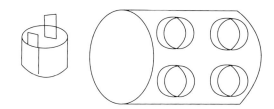

The Neck

1. Draw and cut out a rectangle 6 inches high by $1^1/_2$ inches wide. Fold the rectangle over in half and make a crease.

2. Unfold the rectangle. Measure 1 inch down from the top edge and mark with dots on each side. Connect the dots with a horizontal line. Measure 1 inch up from the bottom edge and mark with dots on each side. Connect the dots with a horizontal line.

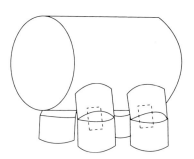

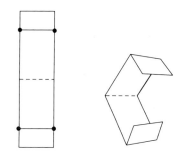

3. Fold the paper on the lines you drew and crease.

4. Form the paper into a triangle by overlapping the two end segments. Glue the overlapping ends together.

5. Glue one side of the triangular neck to the upper part of the covered front lid of the can.

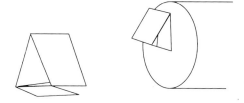

The Head

1. Place a circular object 5 inches in diameter (a full roll of masking tape will work) on a piece of paper. Draw a line around the outside of the object. Cut out this large circle and set it aside.

2. To make the snout, draw and cut out a square $3\frac{1}{2}$ inches high by $3\frac{1}{2}$ inches wide.

3. Measure $\frac{1}{2}$ inch down from the top edge and mark with dots on each side. Connect the dots with a horizontal line. Measure $\frac{1}{2}$ inch in from the left edge and mark with dots on the top and bottom lines. Connect the dots with a vertical line.

4. Cut off the adjoining corner as shown.

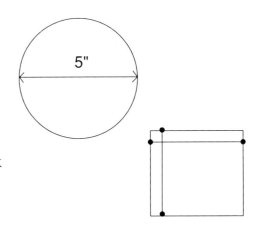

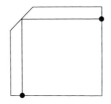 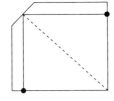

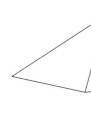

5. To form tabs, fold along the lines you drew. Fold the square in half diagonally.

6. Apply glue to the two tabs. Glue the snout to the lower edge of the large circle as shown.

7. Apply glue to the neck flap and place the circular head in position as shown.

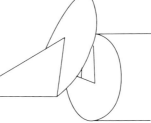

40

The Horns

1. Draw and cut out a piece of paper 4 inches high by $^3/_4$ inch wide.

2. Draw a line connecting two opposite corners of the rectangle. Cut the rectangle in half along this line to make two triangles.

3. Measure $^1/_2$ inch from the bottom on one side of each triangle and mark with dots. Draw a line connecting the dots with the opposite corners. Fold along these lines to form tabs.

4. Apply glue to the tabs and attach the horns to the head, one on either side of the fold.

5. The triceratops has two short horns. Both are made the same way. For the small horn, draw and cut out a rectangle $^3/_4$ inch high by 1 inch wide. For the larger horn, draw and cut out a square 1 inch high by 1 inch wide.

6. Fold the rectangle and the square in half lengthwise as shown and crease.

7. Draw a diagonal line connecting opposite corners on each creased section. Cut along these lines and discard the smaller corner pieces.

8. Apply glue to the horns and glue them to the snout as shown. The short tusk straddles the nose in the middle, and the longer tusk extends off the end of the snout.

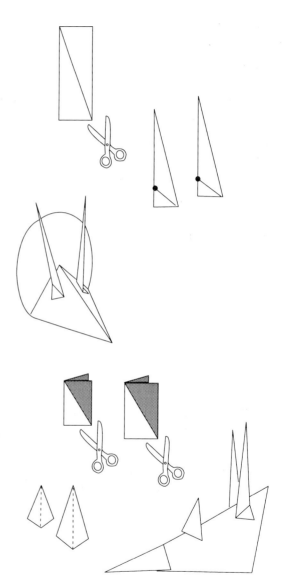

The Tail

1. Don't forget the tail; it's easy to make. Draw and cut out a rectangle 4 inches high by 5 inches wide. Fold the rectangle in half and crease.

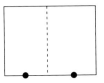

2. Unfold the paper. Along the bottom edge, measure out 1 inch from the folded center line on both sides and mark these points with dots.

3. Draw a diagonal line from each dot to the top of the folded center line to form a triangle.

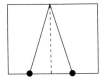
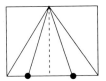

4. From each bottom corner, draw a diagonal line to the top of the folded center line to form a larger triangle.

5. Cut off the areas shaded in the diagram and discard these pieces.

6. Fold the sides of the triangle on the diagonal lines you drew. Form the shape into a triangle by overlapping the end segments and gluing them together.

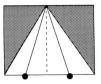
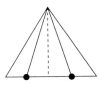

7. Two tips will be standing up from the bottom of the triangle. Bend them down to form a tab. Apply glue or tape to the tab and attach it to the inside upper edge of the body.

How I Decorated:

I gave Trudy's head added realism by cutting triangles and gluing them around the circle. I also cut out and glued triangles to Trudy's feet for toenails. Can you give her some unusual eyes?

Willard the Woolly Mammoth

When we ran past Willard in search of Marbles, we thought we were looking at a woolly elephant from the zoo. At second glance, the long tusks reminded us that we were in a prehistoric world!

44

Let's Begin:

The Body

1. To make the body of this mammoth, trace Figure F on this page onto tracing paper and cut it out. Using this for a pattern, trace the shape onto a folded piece of construction paper and cut it out. (Be sure to place the dotted edge on the fold.)

2. Leaving the paper folded, fold it in half again. Fold and shape this into a three-dimensional tapered triangle by overlapping the end segments and gluing them together. The overlapped side is the underside of the body.

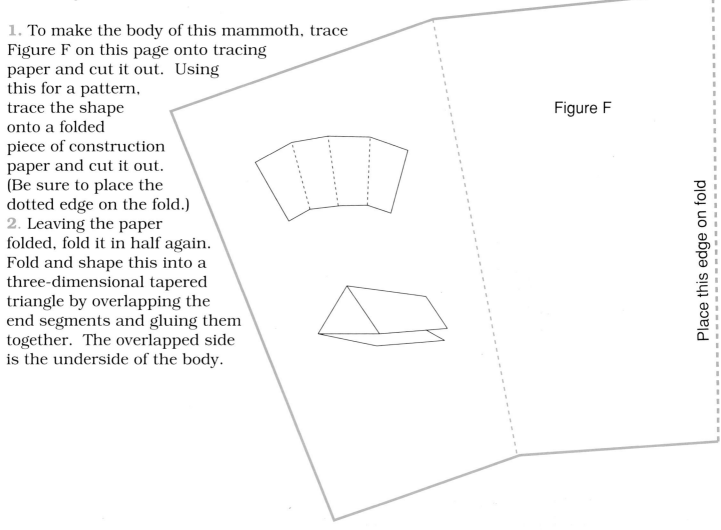

Figure F

Place this edge on fold

The Legs

1. Make a rectangle 4 inches high by 10 inches wide. Fold the rectangle in half and crease, then fold it in half again and crease. Unfold the rectangle and cut it on the fold lines. You will then have four rectangles 4 inches high by $2^1/_2$ inches wide.

2. Fold each rectangle in half. Fold each one in half again. Open the papers and form each into a triangle by overlapping the end segments and gluing them together.

3. At one end of each leg, snip down about $^1/_2$ inch along each fold. Fold back the flaps to form tabs.

4. Glue the tabs to the underside of the body as shown, allowing one of the tabs on each leg to attach up the side of the body.

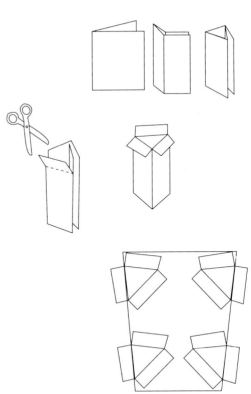

The Neck

1. Draw and cut out a rectangle 2 inches high by 4 inches wide.

2. From the top left corner, measure 2 inches in along the top edge and mark this with a dot.

3. From each bottom corner, measure in 1 inch along the bottom edge and mark each of these points with a dot.

4. Connect the middle dot to the lower dots as shown.

5. Fold on these lines.

6. Apply glue to the outside edges of the triangle's flaps. Slide the flaps into the top corner of the wide end of the body. Hold them in place until the glue sets.

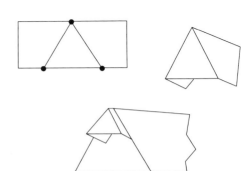

The Head

1. To make Willard's head, trace around Figure G on this page using tracing paper and cut it out. Then place the pattern on construction paper and trace around it. Mark with dots and cut it out.

2. Draw lines on your construction paper piece to connect the dots as in the original pattern. Fold in along each of these lines.

3. Unfold the paper. Form it into a three-dimensional shape by overlapping the end segments and gluing them together.

4. Glue the back of the head to the neck as shown below.

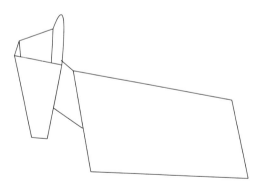

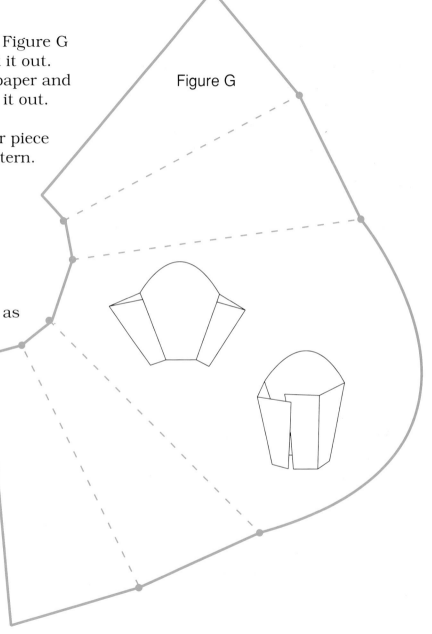

Figure G

The Trunk, Tusks, and Tail

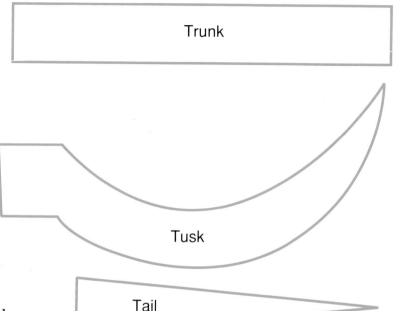

1. To make the trunk, draw and cut out a rectangle $5/_8$ inch high by 4 inches wide. Apply glue to one end of this long, skinny rectangle and slide it up inside the head. Hold the end in place until the glue sets. Roll up the rectangle toward the face and then release. This will make it curl up like a trunk.

2. Willard's tusks are very large. You can draw your own or use my pattern on this page. To attach the tusks, glue the wide ends to the back underside of the head. Then fold the pointed ends forward.

3. The tail is made by simply drawing and cutting a long, skinny triangle and gluing or taping it to the inside back end of the body.

How I Decorated:

I covered Willard with strands of cut yarn to give him an authentic-looking wool coat. I also made big blue eyes by drawing and cutting out circles and then drawing the pupils with a felt-tip marker.

You Will Need:

colored construction paper
pencil
ruler
scissors
white liquid glue
masking tape
18 toilet paper tubes
spray paint—your favorite
   color

Bart the Brontosaurus

This big beast was hard to miss, as you can well imagine! He was one of the biggest dinosaurs that ever roamed the earth. His beautiful 75-foot body made him a sight to behold.

49

Let's Begin:

The Body

1. Bart's body is made with toilet paper tubes glued together in rows. To make the bottom row of his body, glue six tubes together side by side. You may need to hold each tube in place until the glue sets before adding another tube.

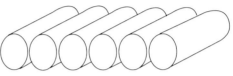

2. To make the bottom-middle row, glue five tubes together side by side.

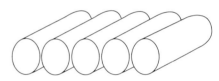

3. To make the top-middle row, glue four tubes together.

4. To make the top row, glue three tubes together. Set all these rows of tubes aside. We will come back to them later.

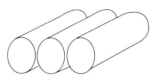

The Legs

1. Draw and cut out four rectangles 4 inches high and $7\frac{1}{2}$ inches wide.

2. Using your ruler, draw lines dividing each rectangle into five sections, each $1\frac{1}{2}$ inches wide. Fold along these lines.

3. From the top edge of each rectangle, measure down 1 inch on each side and mark each point with a dot. Connect these dots.

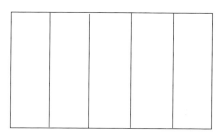

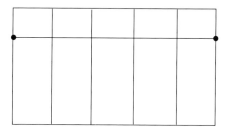

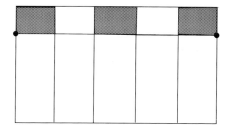

4. Cut out the areas shaded in the diagram and discard these pieces. The remaining sections will be used as tabs later.

5. Now fold each piece into a rectangle by overlapping the end segments and gluing them together. Set the legs aside.

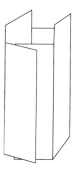

The Neck

1. Draw and cut out a rectangle 10 inches high by 8 inches wide. Fold the rectangle in half and crease. Fold this paper in half again and crease.
2. Open the paper and shape it into a triangle by overlapping the end segments and gluing them together.

3. Now we need to make some tabs. Draw and cut two more rectangles each $2^1/_2$ inches high by $1^1/_2$ inches wide. Fold each of these rectangles in half.
4. Glue one rectangle to each end of the neck so that half of each tab is inside the neck and the other half is outside. These tabs will be used later to attach the neck to the head and the body.

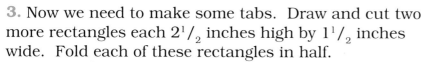

The Head

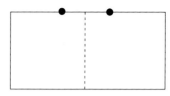

1. The head is made of two three-dimensional triangle shapes. Draw and cut out two rectangles 3 inches high by 6 inches wide. Fold each rectangle in half lengthwise.

2. Unfold each paper. Measure 1 inch on either side of the fold line along the top edge of each rectangle. Mark each point with a dot.

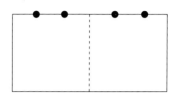

3. Measure 2 inches on either side of the fold line along the top edge and mark each of these points with a dot.

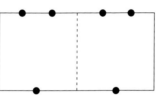

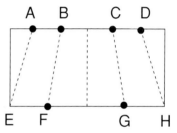

4. Measure $1^1/_2$ inches out on either side of the fold line along the bottom edge of each rectangle. Mark each point with a dot.

5. Draw lines with your ruler connecting corner E to dot A, dot F to dot B, dot G to dot C, and corner H to dot D on both rectangles.

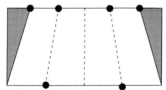

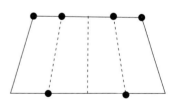

6. Cut off the areas shaded in the diagram and discard these pieces.

7. Fold on each one of the lines you drew.

8. Form each paper into a tapered triangle by overlapping the end segments and gluing them together.

53

9. Place the overlapped sides of the triangles together. Tape the triangles together at the wide ends with one piece of masking tape. This tape forms the hinge of Bart's jaw.

10. At this point you can attach the head to the neck. Apply glue to one of the neck tabs and slide it into the top triangle of the head. Hold it in place until the glue sets.

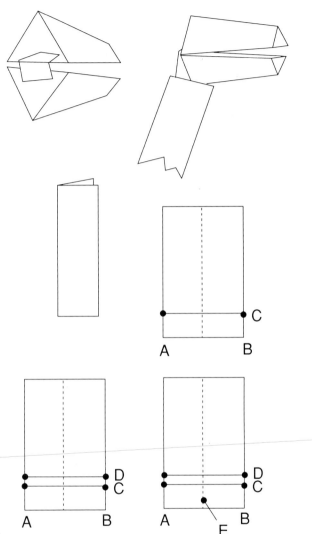

The Tail

1. Draw and cut out a rectangle 12 inches high by 5 inches wide. Fold the rectangle in half lengthwise and crease.

2. Unfold the rectangle and measure 2 inches from the bottom along sides A and B. Mark each point with a dot. Connect these dots with a line. This line is called line C.

3. Measure $2\frac{1}{2}$ inches from the bottom along sides A and B. Mark each point with a dot. Connect these dots with a line that will be called line D.

4. Measure $\frac{1}{2}$ inch from the bottom edge on the center fold line. Mark this point with a dot. This is dot E.

5. Draw lines from the corner points A and B to the top point of the center crease. This makes your first triangle. Then make two smaller inner triangles by drawing lines from point E to the two ends of line D, and drawing lines to connect the bottom point of the center crease with the two ends of line C.

6. Cut off the areas shaded in the diagram and discard these pieces.

7. Cut off the bottom tip as shown.

8. To form two tabs, fold on the two lines you drew to point E. Set the tail aside.

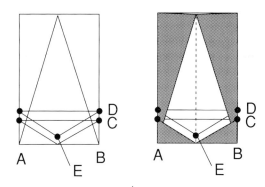

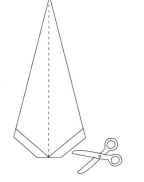

The Assembly

1. Before we actually assemble Bart, we need to spray paint all of his body parts. Make sure you lay down plenty of newspaper to protect the surface you are working on. The mist from spray paint can easily get on surrounding surfaces. Follow the directions on the spray paint can, and be sure to spray all of the pieces. It is important to spray the insides of the body tubes as well. Allow all the pieces to dry thoroughly before you assemble them.

2. Let's start by attaching the legs to the bottom row of six tubes. First fold all leg tabs over. Then fold each leg tab in half.

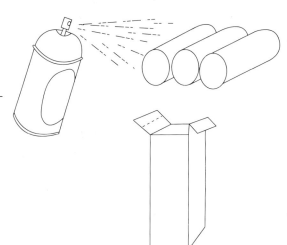

3. Apply glue to the folded tab sections. Place each leg directly on the tubes marked with an X in the diagram. Slide the tab section up between the tubes, and glue the tabs to the adjoining tubes. Make sure you hold each of the glued tabs in place until they set. Now, turn Bart's bottom row over to give him some legs to stand on.

4. Next, attach the head/neck portion to this bottom row. First choose a front and back end. Then glue the lower neck tab to the middle of the top side of the front tube.

5. To balance Bart, glue the remaining tube rows to the body: the row of five tubes on the bottom row, the row of four tubes on the row of five tubes, and the row of three tubes on the top.

6. The tail is the last body piece to be added to Bart. Apply tape to the inside of the tabs so that half the tape is exposed. Apply glue to the outside of the tabs. Now press the tail against the middle rows of the body (those with four and five tubes) until it is set.

How I Decorated:

I used circles, a teardrop shape, and a triangle to make a pair of eyes for Bart the Brontosaurus. You can use your own ideas and come up with something different. Bart has flat teeth. Make the teeth by drawing and cutting four long, skinny rectangles. Fold them in half the long way, and cut notches on one side of the paper just to the fold line. Glue each folded tab to the inside edges of Bart's jaw: one on each side of the top jaw and one on each side of the bottom. What a smile he has now! I also added a curly tongue and some pointed triangle claws to make Bart more realistic.

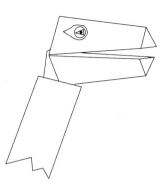

Teeth

Claw

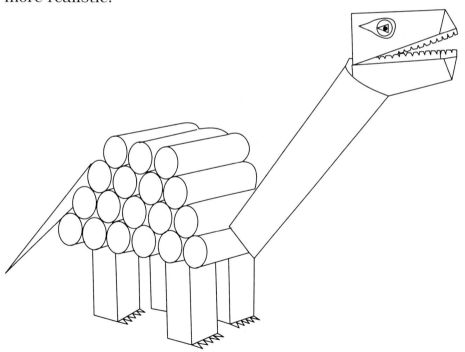

colored construction paper
pencil
ruler
scissors
white liquid glue
masking tape
paper punch
1 15-ounce clean can with
   1 lid removed
2 paper fasteners
1 medium-sized nail
1 wire clothes hanger
hammer
wire clipper

Tyrannosaurus Rex

Of all the creatures we found, Rex was the most
ferocious. Even his name, which means "tyrant
lizard king," sounds menacing.

Let's Begin:

The Body

1. Draw and cut out a rectangle $4\frac{1}{2}$ inches high by 11 inches wide. Glue the short end of the rectangle to the side of the can and wrap it around the can. Attach the other end with glue.

2. Place the end of the can on a piece of paper, and draw a line around the outside of the can. Cut out this circle, and glue it to the attached lid of the can. Remember that the bottom lid has been removed.

The Legs

1. Each leg has an upper, middle, and lower section. To make the upper sections, draw and cut out two rectangles $2\frac{1}{2}$ inches high by 4 inches wide.

2. Measure $\frac{1}{2}$ inch down from the top edge of each rectangle along each side, and mark these points with dots. Connect these end points with lines.

3. Fold each rectangle in half. Fold each one in half again.

4. Open each rectangle. Cut out the area shaded in the diagram and discard this piece.

5. Form each rectangle into a triangle by overlapping the end segments and gluing them together. The rectangle sticking out of the top of each triangular segment is the tab. Set these upper leg sections aside.

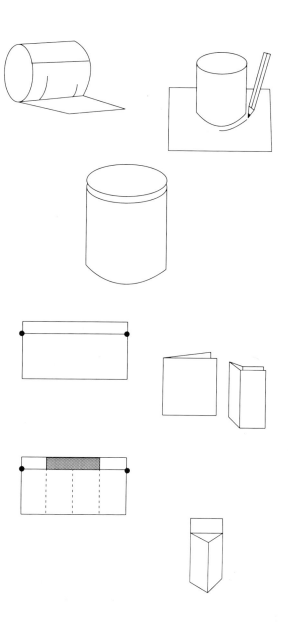

6. To make the middle leg sections, draw and cut out two rectangles 2 inches high by 4 inches wide. Fold each rectangle in half lengthwise. Fold each one in half again.

7. Open each rectangle and form each one into a triangle by overlapping the end segments and gluing them together.

8. To attach the middle leg sections to the top leg sections, take an upper leg section and apply glue to the side of the tab that faces the inside of the triangle. Glue the tab to the inside of the middle leg section. Repeat with the other leg.

9. To make the lower leg sections, draw and cut out two rectangles 1$^1/_2$ inches high by 4 inches wide. Fold each rectangle in half. Fold each one in half again.

10. Open each rectangle. Measure down $^1/_2$ inch from the top edge on folds A and B, and mark each point with a dot.

11. Cut on folds A and B to the dots you just made, and fold the paper down to make a tab.

12. Measure up $^1/_2$ inch from the bottom edge of the paper on fold line C, and mark this point with a dot. Draw a line from the dot you just made to the bottom right corner. Draw another line from the dot you made to the bottom of fold line B. Now measure up $^1/_2$ inch from the bottom on the outer left side, and mark this point with a dot. Draw a line from the point you just made to the bottom of fold line A. Cut out the areas shaded in the diagram and discard these pieces. Repeat this step using the second piece of paper.

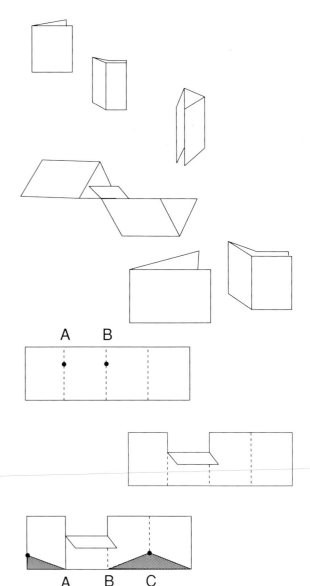

13. Now shape each piece into a three-dimensional triangle by overlapping the end segments and gluing them together.

14. To attach the lower leg sections to the middle leg sections, apply glue to the outside of each lower leg section tab, and slide each tab up into each middle leg section. Press to the bottom of the middle section.

15. To attach the legs to the body, measure in 1 inch on each side from the open-ended bottom of the can, and mark these points with dots. Puncture the can with a hammer and nail at these dots. You may want to ask an adult to help you with this.

16. Paper-punch a hole about $\frac{1}{2}$ inch from the top of the upper leg sections. Push a paper fastener from the inside to the outside of each leg and then through the holes you made in the body. Secure the fasteners.

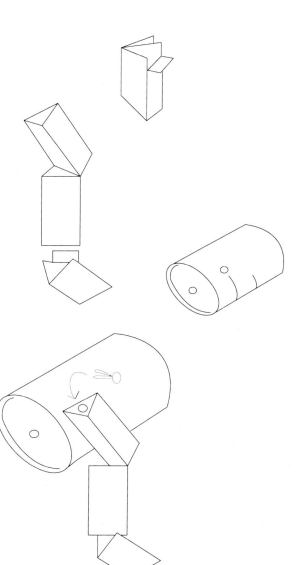

The Neck

1. Draw and cut out a rectangle 4 inches high by 8 inches wide. Fold the paper in half. Fold the paper in half again. Open the paper and lay it flat.
2. On lines A, B, D, and E, measure 2 inches up from the bottom edge of the rectangle, and mark each point with a dot.

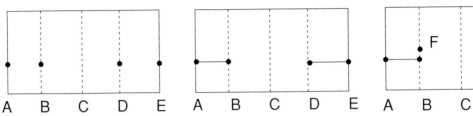

3. Connect dots A to B and D to E.
4. On fold lines B and D, measure up $1/2$ inch from each of the previously marked dots, and mark each point with a dot. These are points F and G.
5. From the top edge of the rectangle on fold line C, measure down $1/2$ inch, and mark this point with a dot. This is dot H.
6. Connect all the dots as shown: dots F and G to the top of line C, lower dot on line B to dot H and F and, lower dot on line D to dot H and dot G. Cut off the areas shaded in the diagram.
7. Cut off the tip of the top point as shown.

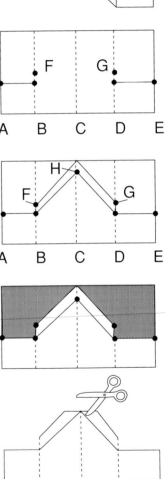

8. Shape the remaining paper into a triangle by overlapping the end segments and gluing them together.

9. Make tabs to connect the neck to the body by folding the remaining two flaps on the triangle shape inward.

10. Apply glue to the two tabs, and fasten them to the covered front lid of the body. Hold them in place until the glue sets.

11. Make one more tab that will help in attaching the head to the neck. Draw and cut out a rectangle 3 inches high by $1^1/_2$ inches wide.

12. Fold this strip of paper in half, and apply glue to one of the halves. Slide this glued section into the neck and attach to the overlapped side. Allow the other half of the tab to extend beyond the end of the neck as shown.

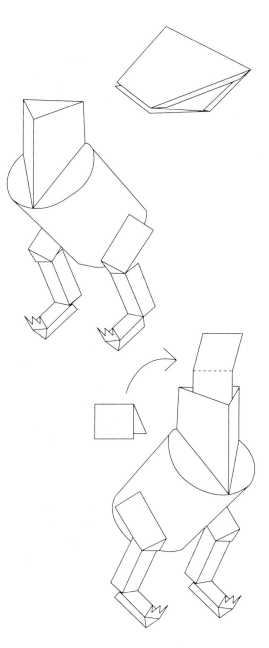

The Head

1. The head for Rex is made in the same way the head is made for Lydia Leidyosuchus. Follow steps 1 through 7 on page 34, but rather than making just one tapered half circle, make two.
2. Tape the head sections together with masking tape, flat sides next to each other.

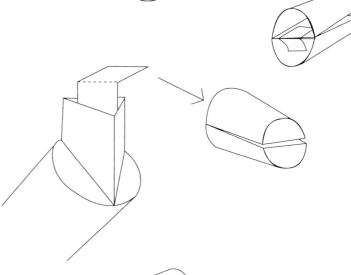

3. Apply glue to the extended neck tab, and slide the tab into the top section of Rex's head. Hold this in place until the glue sets.

The Tail

1. The tail is made by drawing and cutting out a square 8 inches high by 8 inches wide. Roll this square into a long cone shape so the open end of the cone is about the size of the can's opening.
2. Glue the cone at the overlapped ends, and hold it firmly until the glue sets.
3. Take the cone and apply glue to the outer edge of the open end. Slide this glued section up into the body about 2 inches. Hold it until the glue sets.

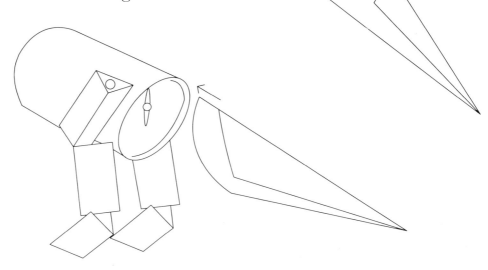

The Arms

1. Draw and cut out two rectangles $1/2$ inch high by $2^1/_2$ inches wide. Fold as shown and attach to the body.

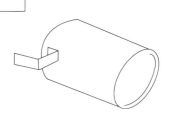

The Stand

1. Using a wire clipper, cut off the hooked end of the hanger. Twist the wire to secure the ends. You might want to ask an adult to help you with these steps.
2. Grasp each side of the hanger and bend the hanger in half, bringing the two sides together. Then turn the hanger upside down so the twisted wire end is at the bottom.
3. Slide the top of the stand into Rex's body just under his tail.

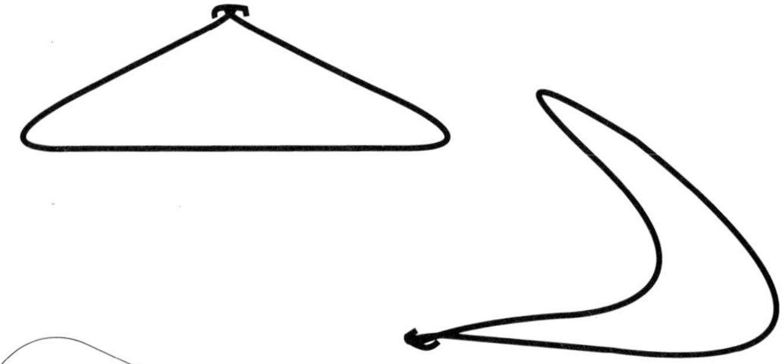

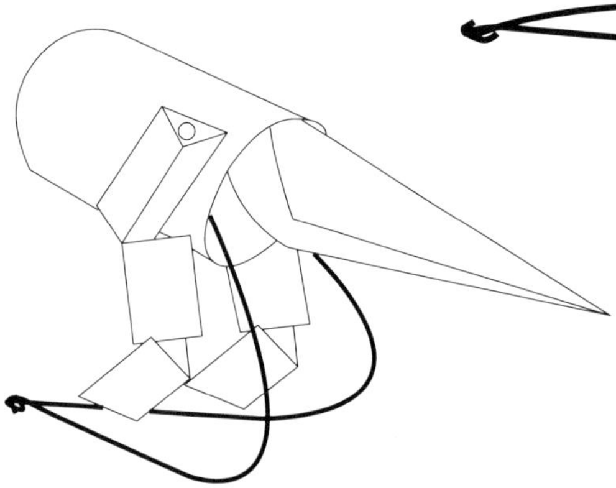

How I Decorated:

I have made hands and feet for Rex and provided you with the patterns to trace. I also gave Rex eyes, sharp teeth, and a curly pink tongue. He actually looks pretty friendly!

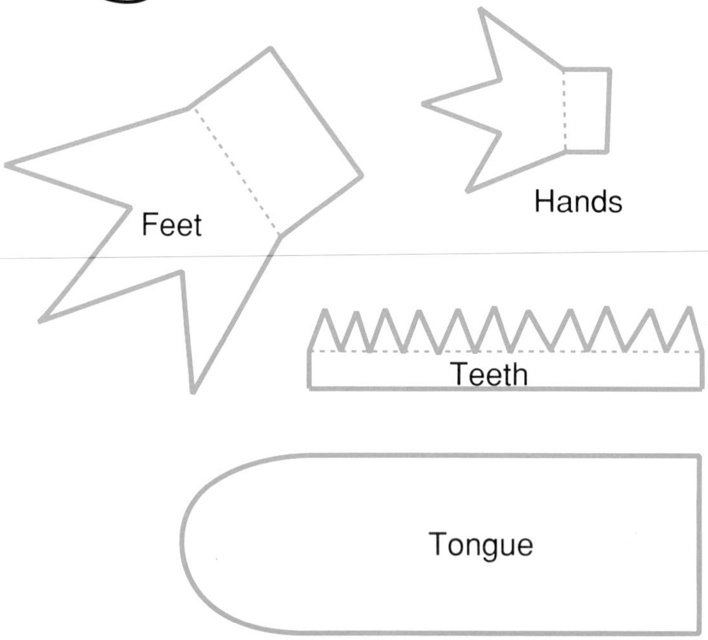

Feet

Hands

Teeth

Tongue

colored construction paper
pencil
ruler
scissors
white liquid glue
1 10-ounce clean can with
  1 lid removed
tracing paper

Prehistoric Plants

The plants in this prehistoric world are as
spectacular as the dinosaurs.

Let's Begin:

The Tree

1. To make the trunk, draw and cut out a rectangle 5 inches high by 4 inches wide. Fold the paper in half. Fold the paper in half again.
2. Open the paper and shape it into a triangle by over-lapping the end segments and gluing them together.

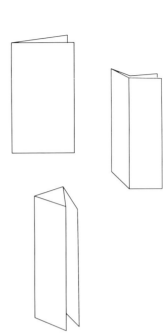

3. Draw and cut out a rectangle 3 inches high by 4 inches wide.
4. Draw a line 1 inch down from the top and another line 1 inch up from the bottom. Cut on the two lines you drew to make three strips.

5. Fold and glue each strip into a triangle as you did in steps one and two.
6. Glue the overlapped side of each of the three small triangles to the sides of the taller triangle at its base.

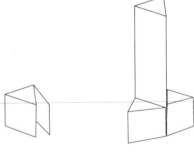

7. To make the tree's leaves, trace the leaf on this page on tracing paper and cut it out to make a pattern. Then trace around the pattern on construction paper and cut it out. You will need to do this twelve times for the leaves.

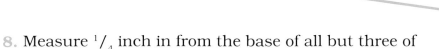

Leaf

8. Measure $\frac{1}{4}$ inch in from the base of all but three of the leaves and fold to make a tab.

9. Glue the leaves together as shown, using four leaves per section. Take an unfolded leaf and measure $\frac{3}{4}$ inch in from the base. Draw a line. Place the fold line of a second leaf at this line. Glue the two leaves together with tabs down. Glue a third leaf underneath the second leaf, where the tab ends. Glue a fourth leaf underneath the third. Repeat this process with two other sets of four leaves.

10. Glue the tab of the bottom leaf to the inside of the trunk so the leaves are facing out. To make the leaves look realistic, you can curl them around your finger to make them curve.

The Bushes

1. To make a base, draw and cut out a square 4 inches high by 4 inches wide. Fold the paper in half. Fold the paper in half again.

69

2. Open the paper. Draw four diagonal lines from the bottom corners to points A and B, and from points A and B to point C as shown.

3. Cut off the areas shaded in the diagram, and discard. Cut on the diagonal lines you drew to make three triangles.

4. Glue the backs of the three triangles together so the folds are back-to-back.

Leaves of the Bushes

Use your imagination to make leaves for the bushes. Then glue them to the base. I used a diamond shape with cutouts and long, skinny rectangles with circles glued on the ends. Mix colors and shapes together to create interesting plant life.

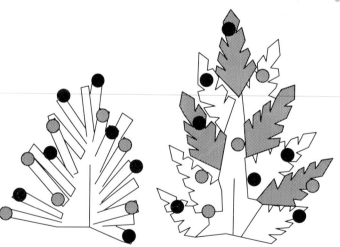

The Flowering Shrub

1. To make the flowering shrub, draw and cut out a rectangle 4 inches high by 10 inches wide.

2. Glue the short end of the rectangle to the side of a 10-ounce can and wrap it around the can. Fasten the end with glue.

3. Using colored construction paper, cut long, skinny strips of varying widths and lengths. You can round the edges, or you can cut them at a diagonal or straight across. Add dots, funny shapes, squares, whatever you want. Glue these shapes to the outside upper edge of the can.

4. Cut out five strips of paper $1\frac{1}{2}$ inches high by 10 inches wide. Use a variety of colors. Make small cuts about halfway down the strips of paper. These are the leaves.

5. Starting from the top edge of the can, glue one strip around the can with the leaves facing up. Glue another strip underneath the first one. Repeat with the remaining strips. Fold and crinkle the leaves in different directions and angles.

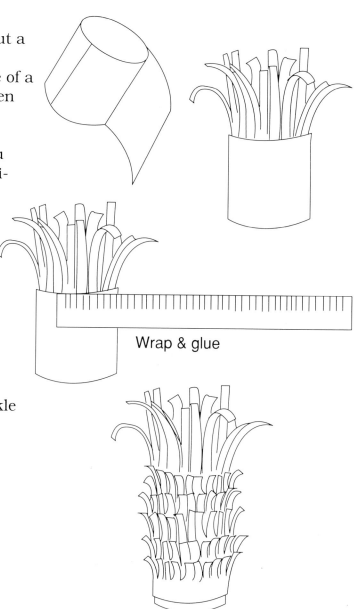

Wrap & glue

71